Ruminations of Ipome

Kenneth Usongo

Langaa Research & Publishing CIG
Mankon, Bamenda

Publisher:
Langaa RPCIG
Langaa Research & Publishing Common Initiative Group
P.O. Box 902 Mankon
Bamenda
North West Region
Cameroon
Langaagrp@gmail.com
www.langaa-rpcig.net

Distributed in and outside N. America by African Books Collective
orders@africanbookscollective.com
www.africanbookcollective.com

ISBN: 978-9956-791-82-8

Dedication

Dedicated to I.A. Usongo: An exemplary father

Table of Contents

Foreword

Kenneth Usongo's maiden creative work, *Ruminations of Ipome*, is a reflection of the life journey he, like most of his contemporaries, has undertaken. These pieces are unique in their ways as each of them embraces a different theme and uses language and imagery that are personal, private and "sacred" to the poet to give the work its unique identity. The poems span the American continent as well as his native African continent, bridging this huge conglomeration of cultures into one continuous experience of humanity. This breadth and depth gives the work its versatility and availability, for it has something to offer all the readers, something to identify with or to recognize, to contemplate or to wave away, to embrace or to shy away. His experiences captured in these pieces and the projections of his imagination render some readers' anxieties less palpable as they measure their own states of mind with the protagonist's.

Crafty in the language of the people and written in a tone that combines the hushes of betrayal, the jubilation of celebration, the victory of life, the frustration of defeat, the exhilaration of new found love, the disappointments of great political expectations, and the failure to carve a personal niche in a global society still in the thralls of a Yeatsian gyration, Usongo's poetry transcends place, time and nationality. I will strongly recommend this book to lovers and students of the human soul, and as a window to the other world, which is both alien and immediate.

Emmanuel Ngwang
Jarvis Christian College
Hawkins, TX 75765
February 24, 2014

Preface

Ruminations of Ipome primarily demonstrates my poetic expression of emotions towards my father and artistic muse, I.A. Usongo, who transitioned to the next realm of life in 2010. In this poetry collection, I have attempted to transcend his mind, posthumously representing his thoughts, feelings, and world view. My artistic endeavour has been guided by the will to recapture his perception of love, nature, family, people, and other aspects of life.

The placing of some poems under specific sections in this book is not hermetic, because some of the poems may as well be grouped under different poetic segments simultaneously. For example, although "Takumbeng" is categorized under people & places, it can also conveniently fall under the rubric of culture. In other words, my placement of a poem under a particular fragment is essentially the result of dominant features evident in the poem.

Loss & Love

Ipome

Lit your face was whenever we were around you
Testament of joy and pride
Amianang[1] you were known to kids
Pala pala, pala pala
Dance
Pala pala, pala pala
They greeted you

Integrity
Sociable
Admirable
Adorable
Clairvoyant

Pioneer in your every enterprise
Indomitable in spirit
Indefatigable in endeavour
Chairman
Teacher
Judge
Councillor

Infectious were your jokes
Community mentor and educationist
You are my rock and inspiration
We mourn and we delight
For your gift of life
For your frankness, honesty, and discipline
A man of your word
Proud am I of you on tree tops, valleys, and mountains

Broom, rake, cutlass in hand
Early morning sweeping and cleaning whistling
These tasks translate your systematic vision of life
You taught me all except how to live without you
Now free you are of anguish
But beaming as your legacy lives on

Our spiritual connection with you remains engraved in our minds
We muse on your love
We muse on your acuity, kindness, understanding, tenacity, ardour
You pushed us, testing limits
Of intellect, love, and grace
In your infancy you bartered cocoyam for "I chev"*2
Tiny may be our voices
In the firmament you grin
As we tread in your trail

The void you have created
The love we miss by your absence
Our hearts forever with fondest memories of you
Thou shall not question God
Good an earthly fight you fought
Favour you have in His eye

Forever miss love
Today is tomorrow

*1 Swallowing cocoyam
*2 Reference to a few English words

4

Weighted Memories

Every day brings weighted memories
Of your cheery outlook and beaming face
Every night brings fresh memories
Of your sanguinity and sensibility
Fond memories of your infectious jokes
Every day fresh with your genuineness and generosity
Every hour makes us better humans
Every minute is weighted by your decency and discipline
We plough into your trove of wisdom
Of stories, persons of yore who aspired and inspired
Your selflessness and sensitiveness drive us on
Sanitizing our raw emotions
Sublimating our thoughts
Chastened by your spirit
We strive and thrive in your drive.

We Remember

We remember your lament about moral erosion in humans
We remember your taunt on kids
On hot cooked cocoyam scalding their lips
We remember your flair for humour
Food never rebels against the mouth
About a couple consuming a full goat
We remember your dedication to pedagogy
Moulding minds at the elementary level
We remember your indomitable spirit
Proud in dignity and humility
As you raged against superciliousness
Daring upstarts to ground themselves
In principles of humbleness and hard work
Integrity at stake let the devil wake up
We remember your audacity in standing up
Against false apostles who inflicted terror on their kindred
Perceptive and pre-emptive
You railed against self-proclaimed messiahs
We remember your sense of camaraderie
Stretching a hand of fellowship to friend and foe
Neighbour and stranger
In the spirit of fraternity
Sunrise to sunset
We remember we remember.

Down by the hills and valleys of Njembeng

Down by the hills and valleys of Njembeng a child is born
Nurtured and livened he was by the wintry harmattan and
pelting tropics
Moulded he was by the chores of tilling and tapping
And acculturated he was by folklore and the *ndek*

Down by the plains of Eba
Lamb-like he drank from the spring of knowledge
By the plateau of Ebab, Mohagmo, and Meta
He refined and defined his vocation

Down by the plains of Eba
He flamed little minds
Deep and determined they mined his ore
Of lore, love, and allure

Down by the hills and valleys of Njembeng resides him
A tree primed with plums
Serene and sanguine of footprints in his trail
That all may pause and ponder.

Muted Voices

the grief-stricken alleys of *inyibad*
strewn by the petals of flowers and leaves
flaunting their somber faces skyward
in remembrance of your feel and favour
huddled together in harmattan they await you
for their sojourns in farm furrows
or beneath the trunks of plantain trees

the air is weary and eerie
leafy branches drip water
the abode desolate and dreary
doors ajar and agonizing
contrite by the absence of the mellifluous whistling
that regenerates and rejuvenates the landscape

the flora dies and is reborn
rain and sun succeed each other
crisscrossing of familiar and unfamiliar faces
all lacking the constancy of one
gentle, gracious, and infectious
the permanence of the patio
the steadfastness of the home and hedge
speak of you today, tomorrow, and forever.

On Crossing the Threshold

Model of meekness and modesty
You triumphantly traversed mundane turmoil of flesh and
spirit
Your religiosity and tenacity the anchor
Tis still fresh in the mind how in an iron bird
You spread the Good News in Akwaya
Like the cascading falls of Egiakoh
You wedded faith with fearlessness in your endeavours
Always a step ahead of your generation.
Tell Ijinjing, tell Abaufei that the seeds are sprouting
Let Etabah and Abu Ano know that the roots are rooted
And Forkwa, Tugwa, Ngebe be informed that the torch has
passed on
The shimmering light scintillates every crevice
Let you and them constantly nudge our spirits
Till ours and yours subsume forever.

Reminiscence

Bland huckleberry cannot seize our appetite
May hot cooked cocoyam peel your back
Then thy name becomes swallowing cocoyam
Juveniles plagued by figures in the turbulence of modernity
Some resolving life challenges with the posterior
In the middle of the river bed
Fifty years to the past and fifty staring at us
Chicken deliciously prepared by a poisoned hand
Finds its abode in the lavatory
That's how bad humanity can be
Some handwriting like a hen scratching the earth
But then seasoned palm wine can preoccupy the mouth
Consumed in excess the mouth becomes restless
Like one possessed by a spirit
Making you an *achatawa**
Although you pride in a grasshopper
Aim at capturing an antelope.

*Disreputable person

You are not gone

You are not gone
Because you are the hissing wind that blows in my face
Because you are the gentle August rain
Because you are the soothing early sunrise
Because you are the radiance of the rainbow
When I wake up every morning
You are the cheerful sound of the robin
You are the soft sound of the broom on the verandah
You are not gone
Because you are the beaming moon in the sky
And you are the sprouts of an April farm.

The Cradler

Repository of laudable personal and family values
Undaunted in your drive to touch every heart
To the community you serve as model
Harnessing their virtues to uplift humankind

Objective in your vision that is
Grounded in selflessness and fulsomeness
We flutter round you like butterflies
Enchanted by radiance of character.

The Hawk

Symbol of the family's coat of arms
As they confront worldly challenges
Swift of foot and daring in feat
The hawk paces without retreating
Engaging daunting duties for its noblesse
Eyes focused on its mission
Its strength and pride shine through its enterprise
Undeterred by its detractors
It roams reassuringly across the sky
Relishing further exploits to stretch its frontiers
Of power, pace, and pride
From its forbears the hawk rarely slumbers and slips
As it flaps its feathers to fan fortitude and foresight in its
kind.

Moments

Moments of anxiety held me
Moments of nostalgia plagued me
Moments of expectation troubled me
Moments of love gripped me

Moments of the past haunted me
Father spoke like a prophet
Ancestor talked with certainty
Friend had long envisioned moment

Still moments of uncertainty clouded me
As I pen these thoughts
Each moment jostles me as I dream the moment
When book and love shall unite for eternity.

The Vision

Sunny weather it was
Beacon of emotions
Setting Eden and auspicious
Instead relics of love flooded my mind
A nightmare of yore it was
As I stretched my arm to catch the maiden
Anguish greeted me

I saw a delicate mango face
Scintillating rays of romance
Smart of foot and lonesome of eye
A smile she wore on the face
As I edged my hand to clasp the maiden
Anguish derided me

Was it real or a vision?
A bright ray of light trailed my window
I stared and stepped on it
It broadened and laughed at me
In a flash, anguish overcame hope.

The Search

One and twenty seasons I searched
Stones I upturned and in streets I sought recreation
Pubs and squares I visited
In search of Divine's creation

Futile seemed the dreary and exacting task
Optimism appeared to bow down to pessimism
Should I relent or should I pursue the endeavour?
Pessimism wrestled with optimism

A prize indeed it was
Exquisite in beauty and radiating comfort
The maiden truly was.
Was the wait worth the patience?
Like the legendary lizard
In pride and grace arched my head.

Legs

They came flaunting themselves
Delicate bosoms
Straight limbs
Full systems
Progenies of Gonne

Stung I was by sensation
I raised my head
But the parade was unending
Balked by precepts and doubt
I shielded my flute.

Garnering

My heart raced with anxiety
Thoughts of glee rivaled those of anguish
Regarding where to anchor the vicissitudes of
Time, place, and vocation

Behind the scenes she
Welded thoughts and actions
Love, poise and ingenuity her assets
As she united friends and family in merriment

Three seasons ago I was at the foot of the Rocky
Determined to ascend the peak in search of the academic
fleece
In one hand a testament of my sacrifices and
In the other love and benevolence

Clad in my ebony suit, sky-blue shirt
I strutted in the warmth of friends
With a glow cast over me in reminiscence
Of my beloved

I beamed like an eagle on iroko
As beloved, friends and family made me soar
In my trail joy, wardrobe and love
As legacies of devotion and compassion.

Engo'o

Munificent in your undertakings
Inspirational in mothering
Radiant in your smile
Auspicious in outlook
Blooming in your endeavours
Exuding love and care and
Letting a trail in your step.

Loneliness

Turning and twisting in bed
My mind wheeled in thoughts
Thumping pages of stories
As I nursed my ennui

Six seasons of romance rolled down memory lane
I ached and yelled out as I retraced the pleasant past
In reliving the pleasures of yore
My jaws drooped

Overcome by loneliness and despair
I strove to wed the past and present
Certain that this will overcome my qualms
Still my eyes were drowned in water

I meditated on life
A taper that ebbs away fast
Determined I was to catch the rose
Deeper I sank in the sea of tears.

Nature & Seasons

Where am I?

They bustled with animation amidst peals of laughter
Songs of rap and sentimental filled the air
Memories of romantic weekends echoed on every lip
I was at a night club last Saturday, burning it out with my paramour
Said a female rider
Oh!, did you see April's latest catch? burst another
In the whirlpool of romantic outpourings
I reviewed the meaning of romance

The bus hissed and swayed
Delicately finding its course in the labyrinthine road
Clusters of trees and neatly trimmed meadows
Sprawling huts dwarfed the splendour of nature
Ou vas-tu? popped in my mind
The steady snoring of the bus muffled
The serenity of trees, the glamour of flowers, the radiance of the sun
And the chit-chat of Cupid's disciples reeled my mind

Once I had thought and felt like the riders
Once I was callow and cheery
But now a gulf stood between me and the throng
Their giggles and fun sounded distant to me
Is it otherness, the cultural-age divide
That jars the melody of Venus that they howled
Or is the nightingale singing weirdly to a weird ear
In a wilderness?

Echoes of the Sea

They streamed out of the listless sea
Arrayed in various colours and shapes
Brown, black, white, crimson

On the heels of steady rain drops
They flaunted their delicate bodies and beauty
In the lead position were the ducks
They swayed to the hissing wind
 To the beating rain they marched in files

Above the ducks fluttered the shearwaters
Under the vigil of the seagull as it
Conducted them in parades across the sky
They whistled and sang in response to the chilling rain

I watched in bewilderment
At the bounty of nature
At the feathered race
As they chanted and beamed
To the serenity of trees, to the rumbling of the sky
And to the worries of humankind.

Park Memories

It was a lovely summer Tuesday
Janik and I basked in the splendour of nature
Stretches of never-ending green beamed at us
Short, leafy trees greeted us with incessant hiss
The whistling foliage competed with the dull
Drone of grass cutting machines

In the horizons birds flew in ecstasy
Above the dead still lake
Ducks taunted each other in a display of grin and acrobatics
Dozen of fishing boats plundered the water
In search of sea creatures
Little boys sped across the water in tiny, agile boats
Like shooting stars

The wind incessantly hissed into our faces
Restraining our ears to the melody of seagulls
The lapping of the rippling water
The twirls of joyous fishes
Such commingling of sounds and sights
Cannot but entice the beholder to the totality of existence.

Clusters of trees

clusters of trees shouldering each other
to the indigenes are their life source
the abode of ancestral spirits
nurse of humanity
provider of wood for the hearth
game for the belly
the leaves and stems are the antidote
to bodily and spiritual ailments

across the sea where sky scrapers and trees wrestle each other
clusters of trees shouldering each other
to the indigenes are their pastime
the escape from the tedium of life
where the eye satisfies its curiosity
where heart strings are knotted or tugged

clusters of trees
to one eye it is the forest
to the other eye it is the park
to humanity it regenerates and rejuvenates.

Long Holidays

When the early rains of June start falling
They bring to me feelings of renewal of nature and love
Dreams of the long holidays and fond memories of father,
mother, and siblings
I embrace school chores with ecstasy
No longer do the onerous exams curb my joys
Thoughts of the greenery of the countryside overwhelm me
The corn stalks pregnant with healthy harvest
The soil pumped with delectable fresh groundnuts
The trees covered in a rich foliage of black and red plums
Mango trees limping under the weight of tempting fruits
The air filled with singing of birds
As they flaunt their beauty from one tree branch to another
My mind races towards the awaited long holidays
The moment when tripod fires in kitchens in the countryside
reveal their pleasures
The delectable corn roasting under the heat of wood
The bulging plums laughing loudly on the simmering wood
ash
My mouth waters as I anticipate the time
When family, friends, and visitors congregate
Round a hearth savouring the special pleasures of the rainy
season.

Saturday Nite

Anxious am I of you
A time to shed weeklong drudgery
A time to nestle with Morpheus

As the rain rubs the corrugated roof
It lulls me into sleep
A moment to travel to distant lands
Dreaming of palatial abodes and delectable foods

Behold I find myself dropping into a sinkhole
In vain I try to climb myself out
My heart quakes feverishly
I perspire like one swimming across the Dudum
Suddenly I scramble out of bed
And am greeted by the sleek pelts of the morning rain.

Nightfall

As the day closes its eyes
Giving way to its sister season
Cloaks of darkness descend onto earth
Bringing lull to human activities
In the peace and silence of the night
Humans relive their quotidian lives
Dreaming away time well spent and wasted
Their minds hallucinate about
Bungled and fulfilled dreams
Of ways to amend faded dreams

Burrowed in the thick of the night
Wake up time for hoodlums
Pondering plots of misery and mischief
Forging plans to disrupt nature
The peace and pace of night on the edge

The barking of dogs
The cackle of roosters
The rumbling of the storm
At these sounds those of no virtue
Tremble like jugs half full of palm wine
Submitting themselves to the righteousness of nature.

Cricket Hunting

With the rains creeping in
Trees regain their allure
Stems ebullient and branches luxuriant
The landscape recaptures its greenery
Refreshing, flourishing and relaxing it is
Like frothing palm wine

The night is cold and charming
At the threshold of their tunnels
Crickets are chirping
With their ebony feathers outstretched
They taunt us with their melody and courage

Guided by our torches
We tiptoe with machetes ready
To bar these seasonal delicacies
From the safety of their abodes

Though often outsmarted by the agility of these insects
Our furtive nocturnal trips
Our giggles, songs, and stories
Compensate for our futile missions
To bring the crickets to the searing pot on the tripod.

Grasshoppers

Harmattan is here
Its sober solemn look
Chills human bones
Deprives vegetation of lushness
Trees and landscape have lost lustre
Like an orphan child fed by a grudging stepmother

Time for the egrets to roam freely the sky
Time for us to savour the blessings of the season
Perching in hordes on every tree and blade of grass
The grasshoppers have lost their vibrancy
Like creatures in purgatory their future is in doubt
Children and adults avail themselves of nature's bounty
Seasoned and spiced they are
A treat of the harmattan
A dessert to spark conversation.

Death

Voices fought for air time
Desolation here and shrieks there
Death in every clime
The frown on a goat's face
Cannot prevent it from being priced at the market
I shrived myself
Walking in a zigzag mood
Crowds wailed in agonizing tones
The night bird raged on
Hearts heavy and men moaned
The mad cow raced at everything
And humans and beast and trees fell
As death spread its long wing
It pulled the vicious into hell
I saw death weary and desolate
As humankind now to virtue relate.

Christmas

Christ
Clothes
Hymns
Food
Wine
Dance
Itchy throats
Whetted appetites
Pleasant flavours
Of chicken, fish, and goat
Kitchens emit tantalizing smells
Houses adorned with trees and cards
The sun beams in joy and praise
The trees have shed their foliage
The horizon looks distant and clear
The mountains are dreary, aged, and enchanting
Birds chirp in bliss and animals shiver in ecstasy
The wind whistles and hisses in the face in symmetry with the
collective trance.

Sunday

Chirps and cackles of birds
Arrows of light
Voices of the faithful
Lull of labour
Welcome you

Mirth and merry in houses
Crates of wine and bowls of food
Bodies make contortions
Sounds pierce the air
In praise of Sunday
Confined in solitude
Stung in the neck and posterior
Aching from pain and desire
I pined in bed
Misery and gloom my companion

Though Sunday it was for many
In vain I strove to grasp any.

Forlorn

It's four o'clock
The horizon is dark and dull
The hills gloomy and weeping
The weather chilly and teary
The sky pregnant

My home is gaping and icy
No streaming images
No sofa
No object of fancy

Only a little talking box
As I guard this lonesome place
Wobbling my eyes to spot humankind
My heart is forlorn
In the grip of expectation
Tears flood my eyes.

Culture

The Squirrel

Though small of stature and not revered
You are smart of foot
Nestled in a shrub or in a foliage of leaves
You hold the key to knowledge
Many flock to you when misfortune strikes them
When fingers are pointed at each other
Or tongues wag out of rhythm
When we have misgivings on anything
Death, accident, sickness
We seek your counsel
Ancient as the hills around you
You have delivered your verdict fearlessly
To the old and the young, the rich and the poor
You have been steadfast in your ruling
Dashing out of the treetop to vindicate innocence
Or diving into the recesses of the forest
To awaken a blighted conscience.

The Rooster

In this age old community still untainted by the slings of
modernity
With trees and the vegetation lush and fresh
The plains placid, extensive, and inviting
Hills roll into each other beneath a broad blue sky
The wind ceaselessly blows in the face
And the sun beams heartedly over the plains
Dusk catches people huddled in their huts
Nestled round hearths telling stories
Creation myths of the past, legends who saved the people in
times of crisis
Tales of courage, virtue, and precept late into the night

Coco coo . . . coco coo . . .
Like a military drill the village wakes up early morning
Men with machetes women with hoes slung on the shoulders
The village troops enthusiastically to the farms, to their
sustenance, and quotidian life
Isn't it a marvel how the feathery race reminds humans to
make optimal use of time?

The Maiden Spirit

Red brick hut with a thatched roof
The abode of the village maiden
Cradle of fertility and guardian of the farms
The wind whistles past her shrine
Like a rushing rivulet
Age old as the oak overhead it
The eternal maiden is omnipresent
Visible yet invisible
Gourds of palm wine, kola nut, fresh sprouts
Tangible signs of village gratitude
To their deliverer

Every season the village throngs
To her abode
To re-thatch and re-wall it
With supplications
With gratitude
Whoever shows favour
Gets a favour in return.

The Diviner

Half his face painted in clay
The other half covered in camwood
He struts slowly like a masked spirit
Holding inaudible exchanges with esoteric spirits
Head crowned with headgear of exotic feathers
Of vulture, eagle, cock and crow
A dark brown raffia bag hangs loosely on his shoulder
In the rainbow bag clasped firmly in his left hand
Kola nut, cowries, alligator pepper, peace plant
Symbols of his uncanny and unpredictable nature
As he walks the jingling sound from his bags
His mute conversations with invisible spirits
Send shivers down the spines of onlookers
He forges relationships between the living and the living dead
Of peace, progress, and permanence.

Who am I?

Can someone tell me who am I?
I know that I am human, born and nurtured in nature
Armed with the senses of sight, feel, touch, and smell
I wine and dine like all living things

I know how to speak Duala, Mungaka, and Ngie
I enjoy *ekwang*, *akwa*, and *achu* washed with palm wine
I can wear *indwifon* and walk like a king
My raffia bag harbours a cow horn, kola nut and snuff
But who am I?

I can play the *ndek* and drum messages
Dressed in my multi-coloured skirt and assorted headgear
I sway to the rhythm of *Ichibi*, *Asondere*, and *Adene*
Play *Makossa* , disco or reggae and you find me gyrating
But then who am I?

I walk with the springs of an antelope
And strut with grace of a zebra
I speak with the ponder of a horse and the hum of a bee
And laugh like a cock yet bleat like a lamb
Still I know not who I am.

The Pacifier

Fury and muddle in the compound
Children wailing as though it was doomsday
Sounds of broken utensils catch people off guard
The lord has gone berserk
Emotions guiding his reason

Egusi pudding in a delicately knit basket
Shrouded in multi-coloured cloth
Restores peace and harmony
This I am told is the domestic pacifier in the Grassfields.

Atupid *

(For Martha Ndaya)

Your fountains are everywhere in the Grassfields
Libations and divinations must cease without you
Cousin to mbuh* and fitchu*
Spirits that make us happy
spirits that make us tardy
Your milky face smiles in darkness
Your fragrance seduces men to you
They eat you up while you eat them down
You are the kernel of truth
Turning stubborn lips into restless mouths
we divulge and devour in your company
we disintegrate and disrobe at your prompting
You ennoble and dishonour us
Bridging us with the living dead
breaching our decorum and discipline with the living
In your presence we sanctify and revel
in your presence we abjure and implode.

*strong palm wine

Ululations

Early morning in a teeming city
Women haggle over goods in a crowded market
Men whet their throats in overflowing bars
Children play games on the streets
Twelve noon
The city loses its pulse
People pour into the streets
Human activities come to a sudden halt
Like a zoo screams rend the air
There's rattling of empty vessels
Drum beating and jingling of keys
Producing a symmetry of sounds
Ululations for the sit tight tyrant
To listen to his people
To relinquish rulership.

People & Places

Once there Lived a Lady

Once there lived a lady blessed with abundance
Of grace, compassion, love, and bounty
Humbled, righteous, and assiduous she was
Meticulous, understanding, neat, dynamic, innovative
Her compound bustled with life
As relatives, friends, and neighbours routinely flocked there
Some sojourned there briefly while others till adulthood
Though of moderate resources she had
She saw every person as a child of creation
Blessed she was with the art of singing
Her angelic voice rent the air
At church services
At singing competitions

In the face of adversity
She imbued courage and tenacity
Perceiving all things as learning experiences
Of God, of man in the earthly journey
Blessed she was with the gift of life

Although she's embraced a celestial life
Relatives, friends, and neighbours invoke her memory
On how to live, love, and die.

Ngebe

Lean, luminous, and elegant she looked
Eyes patient and perceptive
Each time she scanned the sky
Gentle and gracious in the way she strode the world
Her speech soft and sagacious
But like a silent volcano
She erupted when teased
"Ano mind"
Upon hearing these words
She charged forward like a reindeer
Fuming fury
If words lost potency the truncheon triumphed.

Takumbeng*

At the peril of your virility, progeny, or life
Retrace your way as they approach
Take shelter in some shade
Close your eyes or look in the opposite direction
They look imperious in their walk
Justice is their bidding and with grace they embrace it
The Takumbeng are firm, dignified in their walk
Though elderly they may appear, they instill
Hope and courage in people
They are the unsung heroines of Cameroon's democracy
Their powdery hair a testament of their
Wisdom and righteousness of cause
With sealed lips and serene faces
They look fearless
Sirens accompany their march
As clad in Nature's attire
The Takumbeng are unabashed of their appearance
With synchronized steps in rhythm with their heaving
bosoms
These elderly women send the young and the old, male and
female

*A group of elderly women, in the North West Region of
Cameroon, who often militate against injustice.

Soldiers and civilians scampering for shelter
Protectors of the defenceless
Beacon of justice, custodians of culture
Many look up to you
In pursuit of justice, in pursuit of hope, in pursuit of courage
Canons, red berets, tear gas
Cannot change your resolve
Cannot deter your cause.

The Village Courier

Gentle as a dove he is
A burst of smile occasionally flashes his face
When he's eaten his fill
When he's drunk a calabash of wine
He will walk the frontiers of the clan
Enthusiastically and tirelessly he embraces his endeavours
Running errands for the ordinary folk and
Gratuitously fetching water for the needy
An antelope never saw its like
As he rushes through his tasks
Speed and precision his virtues
Now he's regained his sanity
Talking excitedly about his sojourn in distant lands
Of his friends, wife, and family

Another day brings out his other temperament
Stinging like a bee he is
Mute like the *Feg in the dry season
But like a wasp he takes umbrage
At the least provocation
At the least supplication
Broom, pan, and stool fly in every direction
As the lion in him rages on
Such is his conflicting personality
A man of peace, passion, and temper
Such is the legacy of Jonas.

*a small river

Okakan

Listen as he berates his opponents
Like thunder peals his torrid voice tears through
neighbouring villages
Of his strength and courage
Though feeble and elderly he never stops to boast and boo
First to engage in physical confrontation
First to taunt his adversary
First to be rescued
And first to make up for his lack of stamina
What Okakan lacks in strength he compensates with
rhetorical power

Once he rushed into a fight and got a fright
The wind could knock him down easily
Once the provocative Okakan met more than his match
Within the blink of an eye he was sent crumbling down
Like a boulder rolling down Eteiweit*
But for the intervention of onlookers
He would have been pulp for his younger stronger challenger

Okakan's mouth kept running
Running like water on a slippery rock
He was tactically lying down
Contemplating crushing blows at his challenger
Such was his boast and belief
Making words compensate lack of strength
With one blow he would have battered his opponent
Such fiery words from Okakan caused consternation
As reality and rhetoric collide.

*a steep hill

The Extraordinary Pupil

Hoary as he was huge
Daring as he was academically deficient
Asongtu was aloof to school and deaf to twelve
He went through school without school going through him
He queried his teacher whenever he got failed scores
"How dare you scribble red marks on my script?," he
confronted him.
"Is it with me you want to demonstrate your teacher role?,"
he added.
Asongtu could get away with anything
Using age and rhetoric to his advantage
When his teacher read aloud the class results at the end of
each term
Asongtu always was number 60 out of 60
One time Asongtu's father asked him his rank in class
"I am still in my old house," he replied
This is the way Asongtu made light of his poor performance
When challenged by his mother why he couldn't pass his
exams
He fumed this response:
"Why don't you attend adult school like other women rather
than
critique my performance?"
Bemused and exasperated the parents looked on
At a child grown fearless and fearsome without intellectual
curiosity.

The Parade

Weary and wiry they all looked in appearance
Synchronized and sturdy were their footsteps
They are the remnants of the African war gear against Germany
Millions of eyes watched the ex-servicemen
Trudge to the rhythm of a military tune
Eyes poised and chests thrust
They paraded to the delight of onlookers
"Left Right," "Left Right" shouted the lead sergeant
Their heavy boots thumping the turf
They marched beyond the ceremonial grounds
Beyond the edge of the field into adjacent farms
Faithful and compliant they followed the orders of their leader
Trampling crops in the farm
Laughing heartedly the sergeant said
"I forgot the words About Turn"

Unoh Market

Hemmed between two towering hills
Spread like a broken calabash in a raffia bush
Unoh teems and sways to the rhythm of shoppers
The Feg roars beyond the clan
As neighbouring clans troop to you
Goats, sheep, and cows wail
As they are traded for cash
Glittering palm oil empty into huge jars
Gleaming palm wine flow down whetted throats
Young girls with baskets loaded with groundnuts
Haggle their fortune with excited clients
Waists sway in sweaty bars to the rhythm of *Akarikossa*
Beer glides hastily down undulating throats
Of people now like question marks
They brandish their latest *Ashogge*, shoes, skirts, and headgear
Men, women, and children
To the delight of onlookers
To the blast of musical sounds
To the blaring of car horns
And the twittering of birds
And the neighing of horses
As they watch humans manifest collegial emotions.

Eba

I may be physically distant
Yet culturally connected to you
You modulate my thoughts
You regulate my speech
Turning the literal to the connotative
I shape my gait along the contours of your landscape
I inflect my voice in line with
your rushing rivers, hissing winds, and rattling walks
I mould my character along
the serenity of your scenery, the lushness of your flora
and the purity of your sky
You run in my blood
turning horrid into hope, loss into love
Giving mirth and meaning to existence.

Bamenda

Suspended on four hills
The peak of which looks monstrous
Making travelers catch their breaths
As they descend to you

You are a big bowl
Bright faces here, hands of welcome there
Hospitality is thy garment

I hear you bar your teeth
Flex your muscles
In defence of liberty

From the thick of the forest
To the heart of snowy land
You roar like a lion

Instilling courage in lambs
Living in dens.

Kuyam

Midday in Dschang
The pig is crossing the road
Thousands of stooped heads.

Africa

Africa, Africa arise from the shadow of your underachievement
Arise from the slough of war, from the scourge of prejudice
Awake to the drum of political, socio-economic sustenance
Relive your legendary status of generosity, sensuality, and as the cradle of civilization
Through forums of discussion, mass media outlets, we shall celebrate your achievements
Through cultural exchanges and book clubs, we shall disseminate underreported information about you
By bringing together the elderly and the young, the coloured and the biracial, the informed and the misinformed, blacks and whites
We shall champion you in a global context
From the banks of the Nile to the summit of Kilimanjaro
We shall foster understanding among your offspring
From the caravans in Timbuktu to the heart of the Kalahari
You are endowed with abundance
From the shores of the Atlantic to the frontiers of the Pacific
We shall facilitate valuable discourse on democracy, culture, business, and economics
Between you and the rest of humanity.

Ethics & Politics

Forsaken Dream

I rolled and tossed about in the grip of fortune
Soaked in the beauty and grandeur of dream
Meditating on the twists and turns of life
Caged I was in a distant land

Forever overwhelmed in thoughts of hope
Seduced by far-flung promises of glory
Gold by the street and bills by the tree
Jingling coins strewn along the road

The yield is ripe and ready for harvest
Millions craned their necks at the dinner table
Each with a bowl and ladle for the feast
Feast it was for the tall and not all.

Brighten the Corner where You are

Brighten the corner where you are
Make personal aggrandizement a touchstone
Moral probity, intellectual honesty, and self-reliance your
modus vivendi
In consonance with brightening your corner

Birds shall sing and animals leap in the air
Yonder dreams shall become reality
Surrounding valleys and mountains shall resonate
Provided you brighten your corner

Houses, cars, estates plentiful
Families and friends shall trail your path
Foes and detractors reeling backwards
In reaction to your brightening the corner.

Medal

Merit driven is thy emblem
ever often perceived as marker of excellence
dogged and dedicated we strive for your recognition
aspiring to be exemplary in work and life
letting others follow our footprints.

What's Truth?

What's truth?
Is it big, small, thick or thin?
How do we know truth?
By its smell, feeling, taste, or touch?
What colour is truth—blue, black, white, or yellow?
Is truth permanent, temporary, or transitional?
Does it rust over time?
Is it lodged in specific places under given temperatures?
Among particular people?
Of high or low birth? Rich or poor? Learned or unlearned?
Is it a prerogative of a particular race?
Is it experienced in the same way by blacks, whites, coloured, male, female, transgender?
Is it a privilege of the West, North, or South?
Does truth live within or beyond us?
Or is it visible only to the elderly or young?
Does truth grow or starve in the wet season or dry season?
Nowadays, the more we attempt to define truth the more elusive it is.

Money

When he had money
Friends and relatives were plenteous
They drank and dined daily
He listened to the sweet talk of life
Company and comfort never lacked

when he became penniless
lonesomeness and listlessness were his associates
sorrow and sickness kept vigil over him
by his door and bed
depriving him of love and life.

Repassez Demain

Behind a tall table of files
A lean, weary, foxy gentleman
In a stain draped shirt with overlapping cuffs
Sits restlessly combing through tons of paper
Like a bee he orders and disorders his wares
A composite of opposing emotions wrench him
Rancorous, taciturn, sullen, and bigoted
Cheerful, garrulous, encouraging, and enticing
Rustling bank notes determine which emotion to foreground
Columns of anxious weary public servants in front of him
As he burrows and thumbs through
The dust laden stacks before him
Green for an upward motion
Grey for a downward motion
Hope, promise, and progress
Desolation, acrimony, and retrogression
The bilingual context renders him monolingual
He beams and boasts about his selflessness
In milking the national cow
From which we all draw sustenance.

Everyone
(For Grandpa Peter Mbakwa)

Everyone is challenged to meditate on heritage
To bequeath the new generation
Attributes which inspire and empower
Because this endeavor enriches and ensures
A better humanity.

Portrait of a Land Rover

Sturdy, solid and undeterred in appearance
Panting and perspiring it engages the monstrous hill defiantly
The Rover hiccups and howls as it agonizes to a stop midway
Dizzy and dispirited it reels to the base of the hill
Shaking off some of the burden on its trunk
The Rover whines and screeches as its rear hits the bank with
a stomp
Exhausted it suddenly slumps into a coma
After successive epileptic fits the engine comes alive
Men, women, children, goats, and chickens scramble to safety
As it regains its potency the wheels spit thick layers of mud at
passengers
Then the Rover gasps for breadth farting and stuttering
incessantly
Furious and rumbling anger it reengages the hill
It wails and groans to the joy of onlookers
It grumbles and rumbles steadily to the top of the hill
Daring it for challenging its pride
As king of the road.

The Woodpecker

He looks plump
Fresh and smooth like a tadpole
His jaws filled out
His eyes searching and ominous

He looks kempt
With ebony luxuriant hair
Dark trimmed jacket

He smells sweet
Of soothing mellow fragrance
He speaks like a waterfall
Conflating garrulity with eloquence

He is a perfect woodpecker
Drilling holes into the baobab
That shall crush us all.

The Prophet

With both ears cocked
As he cranes his neck in every direction
Serene and sagacious he looks
He crouches towards the east
Then he swerves towards the west
Holding solo dialogues with interlocutors

Wait a minute
Yaoundé is on the line
I hear rumblings in the sky
You'll be the next . . .
Fear not nothing will change

He was partially clothed in Adam's apparel
His belly bursting from the seams
Held in check by cloth wrapped around his waist
Behind him stood his page with bulging pockets
Prophet dialogued with the esoteric
People pressed and stared wide-eyed at him.

Here They Come Again

Here they come again
In sleek sturdy cars
Sweaty, swearing and chanting calumnies
Kempt, charming, convincing they all seem
Selflessness, sincerity, dignity they do lack
Here they come again
Positioning themselves for positions
Under the tropical sun, under the equatorial rain
Like a circus they chant, chat, and cheat
Every season brings familiar faces with the same ramble
To a half credulous and half righteous multitude
They squirm, squeak, and scream
The deliverer—cynical, comical, and capricious
Scoffs at their antics, agility, and ambitions
Here he comes again
Doling posts, medals, and stools
In frenzy and fright he stretches his hand
Lifting fanatics and sitting them on stools
Far beneath the high table over which
He lords and loots for a living.

The Gadfly

Wise, perspicacious, and humorous you are
Though some people question your sanity, you are Solomon
Wily you appear like an eucalyptus tree
Powerful as you lift jugs of wine with bare hands
I remember your cravings for alcohol
When you stated that alcohol must be consumed
Because it is meant to be drunk
Yet its smell often intoxicates you
And you then spew invectives at everybody
I remember when you indicted a politician
For stuffing a cock in his car with its wings fluttering
I remember when you reproached a *mbere
For being pregnant with a he goat
I remember when you hurled diatribe after diatribe
At your detractors
"If rice were good for human sanity
Why don't you consume it too?"
"How greedy you are like your chickens!"
Beneath your semblance of lunacy
Are embedded wisdom and knowledge
Gracious and eloquent you are
But impertinent upon provocation
You would say to your teasers
"Let the balls not only swell, but they should pain and then explode."
Rock of ages you are
Depository of wisdom and humour
You are to the community.

*mbere refers to a police man

76

Tell me What it is

When mouths yawn in hunger
And vent words of disgust
When bodies ache
And filth invades cities
Tell me what it is

When a lord arrogates power and wealth
Turns his eye when cronies bathe in affluence
When a castle is fortified by barrels
And a palace flowing lust
Tell me what it is

When men numb their senses and sing odes
With tummies overblown
When kinsmen cum Ananias swear truth
And glory in deceit and servitude
Tell me what it is

When a nation crawls under abuse
And a people yell out riddance
When the cream seeks bread beyond the native land
But the crown pursues apathy and entropy
Tell me, tell me what it is.

The Messiah

He filled up his belly with grain
And stuffed his stomach with liquor
But starved himself of modesty
He loaded his pockets with wads of bills
But emptied his head of lore
He craned his neck into the sky
Amidst deafening drumbeats
The soil gave way beneath him
And he was swallowed in it
Ignominy is his epithet
history is written in water.

The Griots

They kept talking
Like a waterfall
Like the whistling wind

They kept singing
Like a songbird?
No, like Babel
Like metal

On on and on
They went
In falsehood
In praises
Of the messiah

They kept sniffing
Like dogs
Like rats
For crumps
For recognition

Prostrate across its triangular abode
The lion flapped its mane
Talk, song, and praise
Left it insensitive
Unnerved
Numbed
To distant catcalls.